BIRDS OF THE WORLD
WATERFOWL

BIRDS OF THE WORLD
WATERFOWL

JOHN P.S. MACKENZIE

NorthWord
PRESS, INC

Copyright © 1988 by Key Porter Books Limited

Originally published in Canada by Key Porter Books, Toronto

Published in the United States by:
NorthWord Press Inc.
Box 1360
Minocqua, Wisconsin
54548

ISBN: 0-942802-94-2

Library of Congress Catalogue Card Number: 88-061092

For a free catalog describing NorthWord's books call 1-800-336-5666

Design: First Image
Composition: First Image
Printed and bound in Italy

88 89 90 01 02 6 5 4 3 2 1

CONTENTS

Greater Scaup (*Aythya marila*)   The Greater Scaup nests from the Arctic
Ocean south to about 60 degrees north latitude. In winter it moves to salt
water where it dives for food. Rafts of thousands of birds are common.

INTRODUCTION

Mallard (*Anas platyrhynchos*)   This is a male Mallard in full nuptial plumage. It is the most widely distributed and common of all the ducks, its range covering the Eastern and Western hemispheres, and extending as far as northern Australia.

The term "waterfowl" is normally understood to include only swans, geese and ducks. For this volume we have added grebes and cormorants which often share the same habitat.

Waterfowl have a number of features in common. All feed to some extent in water. Some, such as the dabbling ducks, geese and swans, feed from the surface. They up-end, with their tails in the air, and stretch their necks to reach food under the surface. The diving ducks submerge completely, and swim under water for their food, sometimes to a considerable depth. Their diet tends to consist of animal matter in the form of fish, molluscs, crustacea and insects.

Six years ago, when we were exploring the arid plains west of the Murray River in Victoria, Australia, we were guided to a shallow lake which was crowded with ducks and swans. After hours of heat and dust, the water and green margins were a restful and relaxing change. There were several dozen Black Swans, indigenous to Australia and New Zealand, Chestnut-breasted Shelduck, Chestnut and Grey Teal, the striking Southern Shoveler and Blue-billed Duck. Altogether, there were over a thousand birds. This lake, the only standing water for several miles, acted as a magnet for waterfowl and the wading birds that dotted the shore. Our visit was during the dry season. When the rains came, the birds would range widely to nest, for the area was too small to support such a population for a long time.

The waterfowl that we saw in Australia migrate only within the country in search of lakes, rivers and marshlands in which to feed and nest. In the Northern Hemisphere, most waterfowl are migratory. In the spring, they leave the ice-free areas where they have wintered in ponds, lakes, swamps, estuaries, and on the edges of the oceans, to move northward. Some wood duck, teal and mergansers do not go very far, but settle in suitable watered areas. Others, including the Tundra Swan, spread out across the tundra of North America and northern Europe, and throughout the vast taiga of Siberia. Still others, including the King Eider and the Oldsquaw, whose ranges extend as far north as there is land on which to nest, press farther, to the limits of the Arctic islands.

Geese, swans and ducks that nest in the Far North are often faced with conditions critical to successful nesting, and to their own survival. Although migrating waterfowl build up reserves of fat prior to their long journeys, they arrive on their breeding grounds in a weakened condition. This is especially true of swans, for example, which make long, non-stop flights, or stop to rest and feed only briefly. Snow geese, in contrast, make long intermediate stops — sometimes as long as a month. If the migrants arrive at the nesting grounds before the snow has gone, or before the ice has left the shores, they may starve. They can, however, survive for two or three weeks, and nest before arctic vegetation has started to grow. The period between thaw and freeze-up may be as short as eight weeks. Since incubation takes from three to five weeks, depending upon the species, and since the young must be fledged before freeze-up, they must grow very quickly.

Waterfowl born in the Far North grow more quickly than those in the south, due to the abundant food supply and continuous daylight. Canada Geese, for example, which nest over most of North America, gain about one pound a week, and may be fully grown in eight weeks in the south. The same process in the Arctic may take six weeks. For this species, it takes approximately 100 days to nest, incubate and raise the young to the flying stage.

The marshes at the margins of rivers, lakes and the oceans which attract waterfowl on their autumn migration are exciting locations for avid birders during the half hour or so before sunrise. Then, at first light, they can hear the marvelous chorus of marsh sound. First, there is the splashing as birds rise from their resting positions and flap their wings. The croaks and cackles of grebes and coots follow. Both species indulge in nervous splashing and grunting in the reeds. There is the occasional feeding quack of a Mallard, and then the rustle of wings as ducks start to move about the marsh. Most species can be identified at a considerable distance by the experienced observer: flight patterns differ, shapes are slightly different, wings beat at varying speeds. Pintails, for instance, have pointed wings and long tails; scaup have a rapid wingbeat and fly close to the water; teal are small and dart about erratically. When it is full light, the drama subsides.

The chicks of waterfowl are "precocial." This means that they are born with protective down and their eyes open. They are also "nidifugous," meaning that they have well-developed legs and are capable of leaving the nest as soon as their down is dry. In fact, they head almost immediately for the nearest water, sometimes a long way off, where they can swim, dive and feed themselves within a few hours of emerging from the egg.

Another feature common to waterfowl is the leathery web which joins the three front toes. The single rear toe is vestigial, usually no more than a tiny spur emerging slightly above the foot on the tarsus. Grebes' feet are exceptional in that they are not webbed, but the toes have lobes which bend sideways when they are swimming, providing added propulsion.

Most waterfowl have short legs and tails, narrow wings and longish necks. Most also have long, flat bills, with varyingly serrated edges, which they use to strain water while retaining food. All members of this group have a complicated system of feathers of which the outer layer is virtually impervious to water. By preening regularly, arranging the barbs on the feathers, and by the application of oil from a gland near the tail, the feathers are kept lubricated.

Ducks, geese and swans are designed primarily for swimming and flying. Their legs emerge relatively far back on the body. This varies among species, as does the ability to walk on land. The dabbling ducks, with legs at the center of the body, waddle quite well, as do geese and swans. The diving ducks, with legs near the rear, are clumsy on land.

Many species of waterfowl, particularly the dabbling ducks, geese and swans, vary their feeding habits between land and water. Geese and swans graze on grasses, seeds and the various clovers. In agricultural areas they eat wheat and other grains in huge quantities. During the autumn migration, large flocks descend on uncut fields and strip the grain from the stalks. The damage can be so great that the fields are not worth harvesting. In the spring, migrating waterfowl may do comparable damage to the young shoots of grain crops. In North America some prairie regions are particularly hard hit; the worst offenders are usually Mallards.

Waterfowl nesting in the Northern Hemisphere tend to migrate much farther than those south of the equator where, for the most part, migration may be limited to the search for suitable habitat. This is usually due to seasonal precipitation rather than freezing. In much of Africa, Asia, Australia and South America, it is necessary for waterfowl to follow the rains, more often east-west than north-south. Several species, including the Black Swan, the Plumed Whistling Duck, the Freckled Duck and the Chestnut Teal, occur only in Australia and New Zealand. Some, such as the Yellow-billed Duck, the Cape Wigeon and the Hottentot Teal, are seen only in Africa. And a few are found only in fairly restricted areas in South America. In some remote islands, such as New Guinea, Madagascar, the Falklands, the Crozet Islands, the Andamans and New Zealand, there are isolated species that occur nowhere else.

During the first half of the twentieth century, counting methods were primitive and the records are suspect. Since about 1950, most wildfowl counts have been conducted from light aircraft with fair accuracy. It has been determined that the North American population averages 40 million birds at the beginning of the breeding season, and 80 million at its end. It does not appear to be declining seriously. The game laws that were first introduced in the United States in 1918 limited the daily bag to 25 ducks. Now the limit has been generally reduced to more modest numbers.

In the early years of the present century, both in North America and Europe, it was not unusual for a single hunter to kill hundreds of birds in a day. North American species still face uncontrolled slaughter when they reach Mexico, which does not enforce the Migratory Bird Treaty. Some years ago in Merida, in the Yucatan Peninsula, I met two North Americans who boasted that on that day they had killed 500 duck.

Natural hazards remain a constant threat to waterfowl populations. Disease caused by blood parasites, botulism and fowl cholera, is probably the largest destroyer. Fowl cholera strikes large bird populations feeding in stagnant ponds, in areas where there is not enough suitable habitat. Periods of drought have a serious impact on the capacity of waterfowl to nest and raise young. Prolonged winters and violent storms kill many young birds. Predators, both avian and animal, threaten eggs and young birds.

Unnatural hazards are increasing, despite solid efforts to control them. Regular shooting by hunters has carpeted the bottom of many marshes with lead pellets. These pellets, ingested by feeding birds, lodge in their gastrointestinal tracts. Some birds can tolerate a few pellets, but when the number of pellets exceeds their tolerance, the birds are poisoned. It is estimated that two to three percent of the fall and winter populations of waterfowl die from lead poisoning. (In many areas, hunters are now required to use steel rather than lead shot.)

Oil spills, in both fresh and salt water, not only poison waterfowl as they try to clean their feathers, but also kill them by destroying their waterproofing.

The nesting habits of waterfowl are generally consistent, in that they lay their eggs as close to the water as they can, although late arrivals and less aggressive individual birds lose out on the best territories. Some ducks are exceptional, in that they nest in uplands away from the water. Most species nest on the ground, or on an elevation in a marsh. Nests vary from a scrape lined with down, to substantial piles for some of the geese.

Pair relationships differ considerably among waterfowl and between species of the same family. Swans and geese pair and tend to remain together for long periods, often for life. Among ducks, pair bonding is strong while it lasts, but is often of short duration. Bonding may take place in the autumn and continue through the winter and migration. With some species, the male attends the female during nest building and during egg laying, but departs when incubation begins. Among other species, the male will remain until incubation is well advanced. Once hatched, the young are capable of feeding themselves, and need brooding only at night and during harsh weather.

Longevity varies considerably. Trumpeter Swans have lived in captivity for 29 years. Ducks' longevity is much shorter. The life expectancy — as opposed to longevity — is another matter. It has been estimated that the average life expectancy of a Mallard in Europe is six months. In North America, the annual mortality rate from all causes, for those species subject to shooting, is about 60 to 70 percent, so the chance of reaching old age is slight. About one half of the mortality is due to shooting; the rest to other causes. Since waterfowl are prolific breeders if habitat is available, they can tolerate relatively high mortality. Swans average five eggs per clutch; geese slightly more. Most duck species average about nine eggs per clutch. Nesting success varies enormously depending upon human interference, predation, and weather, but, on average, less than half the eggs laid produce flying birds.

Throughout most temperate regions, a fast-growing human population has, for centuries, demanded increasing areas of land for agricultural production. Much of this land has been claimed from natural wetlands. With the invention of powered machinery in the nineteenth century, the process was accelerated. In the United States, for instance, there were originally about 127 million acres of natural wetlands. By 1968, this had been reduced to 75 million acres. Much more has been lost since then. In Canada, where vast areas of northern forest and tundra account for some 2.24 billion acres, the losses have not been so great in relative terms, but much of the best of the pothole country and estuaries is being drained. From a human point of view, food production is, of course, essential, but so is the maintenance of wetlands for water storage and natural drainage. Drained land does not hold spring rain or melting snow, and consequently leads to drought conditions in a dry summer. From the point of view of maintaining waterfowl populations, the loss of habitat is disastrous. Recently, it has been recognized that human interference and loss of habitat to agriculture have put pressure on waterfowl populations that may become intolerable. In North America, particularly, an enormous effort in terms of money and research has resulted in the retention and creation of wetlands. This has to some extent halted the decline in the vast populations that once existed.

Whooper Swan (*Olor cygnus*) The trumpeting call of the Whooper gives it
its name. It nests in Iceland, across northern Europe and Asia and moves
south as far as North Africa in winter.

SWANS

Coscoroba Swan (*Coscoroba coscoroba*)   The short neck, white body, red bill, and relatively small size identify this bird. It lives entirely south of the equator from southern Brazil to Argentina and Chile.

Many people tend to think of swans as ornamental birds, because they are usually seen floating majestically on ponds in zoos and botanical gardens. The bird most commonly seen is the Mute Swan, an enormous, all-white bird, with a pinkish bill surmounted by a black knob. This swan has been semi-domesticated in Europe for centuries, and is recognized as a symbol of elegance and grace in myth and legend. Tchaikovsky immortalized it in his ballet, *Swan Lake*. In the British Isles, where the swans nominally belong to the monarch, the wild population is probably descended from semi-domesticated birds of the medieval period. Mute Swans were imported into North America in the nineteenth century for ornamental purposes, and escapees have established themselves in the wild.

Populations of Mute Swans that have become established in some parts of North America, for example on Chesapeake Bay in New England, have caused some disruption to the local environment. They tend to drive other waterfowl out of the nesting territory. They pull up a lot of the aquatic vegetation. And generally, they may be at least partially responsible for a local decline in habitat suitability for other waterfowl.

There are — arguably — seven swan species: Whooper, Trumpeter, Tundra (or Bewick's), Mute, Black-necked, Black and Coscoroba. Some years ago the Whistling Swan of North America was re-named the Tundra Swan. More recently, it was agreed among ornithologists that the Bewick's Swan of Europe and the Tundra Swan of North America were, in fact, the same species. To further complicate matters, some authorities now consider the Trumpeter Swan of North America to be conspecific with the Whooper of Eurasia, although this has not been recognized in official circles. The Tundra-Bewick's and the Whooper both nest across northern North America, in the Arctic islands and in northern Russia. They visit the British Isles in winter to feed in ponds, rivers and protected estuaries. Both are straight-necked birds. The necks of Mute Swans, in contrast, form a distinct S. Finally, ornithologists now maintain that the Coscoroba and Black Swan are members of the duck tribe. I include them here because swans are what they are called and what they look like.

The Black-necked, Coscoroba and Black Swan live only in the Southern Hemisphere. The first two are found from Brazil southward, and the Black in Australia and New Zealand.

In Europe and North America swans, with the exception of the Mute Swan, nest in remote regions and require large territories to themselves. (The Mute Swan of Europe nests quite happily in parks and farmland.) Swans usually choose wetlands in the tundra, or land surrounded by water. Here they build a bulky nest on a mound they have made themselves or, quite frequently, by scooping out the top of a muskrat mound. The Tundra Swan claims and maintains a territory of at least one square mile. It will tolerate duck and other small birds, but drives off most geese and other swans. It is because the Trumpeter Swan requires a similarly large territory that it was driven, by the expansion of agriculture on the Great Plains, to the brink of extinction.

Swans are gregarious outside the nesting season, and some species nest in loose colonies. On a visit to the evaporating ponds of the salt works of Imperial Chemical Industries in Adelaide, Australia, we saw one flock of Black Swans estimated to be more than 1,000 birds. When our host put them to flight, they presented a magnificent roaring display of brown-black bodies and red bills. Migrating swans in the Northern Hemisphere tend to settle for feeding stops of a week or so, as they follow the spring north. Near Chatham, in Ontario, several thousand Tundra Swans litter the fields in March, feeding mostly on last year's corn and some early shoots.

The species particular to the northern part of the Western Hemisphere are the Trumpeter and Tundra swans. The Trumpeter is rare south of Canada, outside the Red Rocks Lakes area near where Wyoming, Montana and Idaho meet. Due to heavy shooting and restricted habitat, the Trumpeter population declined to a low of 69 birds in the U.S. and south of Canada in 1932. Concentrated and intelligent work by federal, state and private agencies has led to an increase in the group to about 700 birds, at which level it remains more-or-less stable. Further expansion is limited by restricted nesting habitat. Another and separate population of Trumpeters, numbering about 3,500 birds, lives in southern Alaska and northern British Columbia. This bird once nested widely and was common throughout the central and northern part of North America, but it could not withstand encroachment and the draining of its habitat for farming.

The Tundra Swan remains abundant in North America and, as its name suggests, nests from the Aleutians, across northern Alaska and the Northwest Territories. Once, when flying westward to Prudhoe Bay in Alaska, we were able to see the nesting birds clearly against the dun-colored tundra. Although swans usually fly in flocks with their own kind, sometimes on migration young swans fly with Canada Geese, usually in the lead.

Swans establish strong bonds and pairs mate for life. They remain together throughout the year, keeping the surviving cygnets, or young, with them until they nest again. If one of a pair dies, the survivor usually takes a new mate, but when they are together their mutual affection (if birds can be said to feel affection) is apparent. Swans and geese carry out mutual displays prior to mating. Aggression displays to intruders involve a lowering of the neck, hissing, and forward rushes. Success in sending off an intruder is heralded by a display of triumph. At the nest it appears that the female does most, if not all, of the incubating of the eggs. The clutch averages about five eggs, but may be as many as 10. Incubation for most swan species is about 30 days. The survival rate of the young is reasonably high during the next 60 to 75 days that it takes them to develop to the flying stage. For those species nesting in the Far North, about half the young birds perish on migration to the south, for they must leave the Arctic before they have grown strong.

Swans of the Northern Hemisphere migrate to their wintering area in flocks of about 20 to 40 birds. In winter they are gregarious, feeding together in very large groups.

Tundra Swan (*Olor columbianus*)   Formerly known as the Whistling Swan, this is a Holarctic species which nests in northern North America and in Siberia.

Left: Trumpeter Swan (*Olor buccinator*) Swans of this species were once widespread, from James Bay to the Mackenzie River in the north, to Nebraska and Missouri in the south. They once wintered as far south as the Gulf of Mexico.

Mute Swan (*Cygnus olor*) This is the swan most often seen in zoos and ornamental gardens. It was introduced into North America in the nineteenth century and breeds in the wild.

Mute Swan (*Cygnus olor*)   This large swan takes off from land or water ponderously, with a heavy flapping of wings, and with its feet pattering along the surface. In bogs it may even be grounded.

Whooper Swan (*Olor cygnus*)   The Whooper nests on firm spots in the Arctic tundra as well as on islets in lakes and bogs. It winters on sea coasts, lakes and large rivers around the British Isles, northern Europe and at the head of the Adriatic.

Left: Tundra Swan (*Olor columbianus*)   Migrating from the Chesapeake Bay area where it winters, to the shores of the Arctic Ocean, the Tundra Swan takes a month-long intermediate rest part way, and then flies non-stop to the Northwest Territories, Baffin Island and Siberia.

Mute Swan (*Cygnus olor*)   Note the long, curving S-shaped neck and the orange, nobbed bill. The yellow stain on the neck is the result of constant feeding with the head below the surface. The raised wings are typical.

Trumpeter Swan (*Olor buccinator*)   Once widely distributed through the
plains of North America, only about 700 birds remain south of the Canadian
border. A separate population of about 3,000 birds lives in British Columbia
and Alaska.

Mute Swan (*Cygnus olor*)   Although gregarious in winter, often gathering in groups of a hundred or more birds, in the breeding season Mute Swan pairs are apt to be isolated.

Black-necked Swan (*Cygnus melancoryphus*) The striking black neck and face, and the brilliant red nob on the bill contrast markedly with the white body. The Black-necked Swan lives only in South America, from southern Brazil to Argentina.

Black Swan (*Cygnus atratus*)   A native of Australia and New Zealand, this swan congregates in large numbers when not nesting. It is abundant in both fresh and salt water.

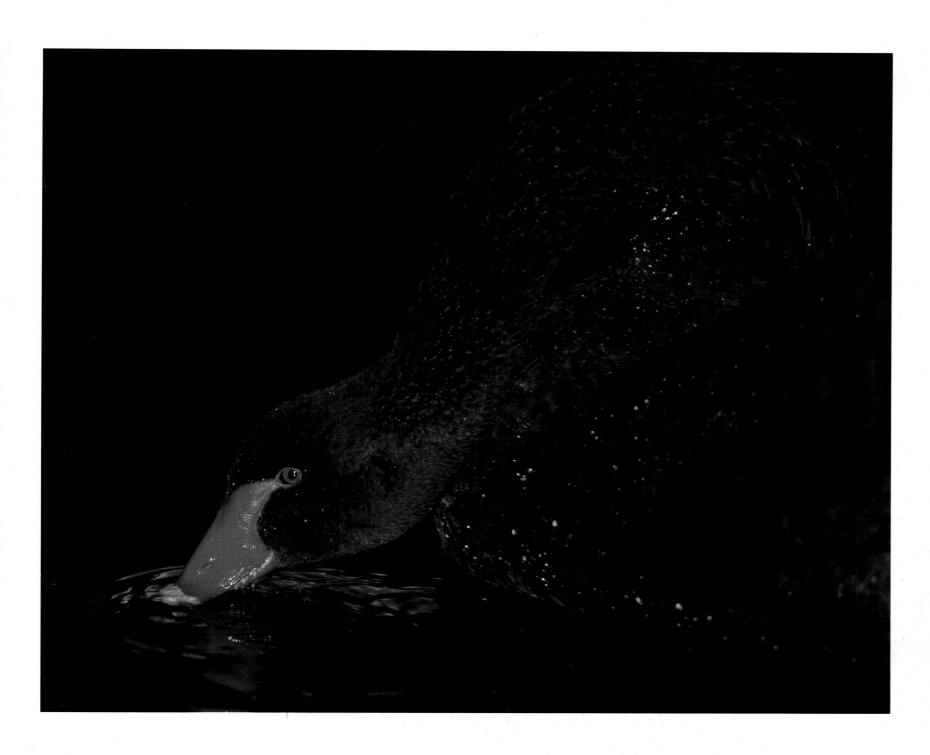

Left: Black Swan (*Cygnus atratus*)   The black-brown color and straight neck are typical of this swan. They lay an average of five eggs, with both the male and the female incubating.

Black Swan (*Cygnus atratus*)   The Black Swan is often found in a pond or small lake many miles from standing water. The white tip on the red bill can be seen for some distance.

Tundra Swan (*Olor columbianus*)   The Tundra Swan chooses nesting sites anywhere from the water's edge to low hilltops as much as half a mile from water.

GEESE

Barheaded Goose (*Anser indica*)   This attractive goose nests, usually at high altitudes, in central Asia and Tibet, laying three or four eggs. It winters in northern, and occasionally central India. It feeds mostly at night and congregates in flocks to rest during the day.

Ornithologists differ in their classifications of waterfowl, but there appear to be about 37 Anserinae species around the world, of which nine fall into the whistling duck category, and 28 are called geese and swans. As an example of the problem of classification, there are five species of sheldgeese in South America that, in evolutionary terms, are more closely related to ducks than to geese. Both sheldgeese and shelducks, however, may be classified as geese.

Geese are intermediate in size between swans and ducks, and tend to have longer and heavier necks than ducks. They are agile on land, where most species do much of their feeding. Their legs are relatively longer than those of swans, and emerge close to the center of the body. They also feed in shallow water, where they up-end in order to reach aquatic vegetation with their bills. Most geese are almost entirely herbivorous in their feeding habits, although some feed partially on insects and shellfish. Geese will adapt to changing circumstances, however. For example, before the European settlement of North America, geese fed exclusively on wild food, probably obtained mostly in the water. With the expansion of grain farming, geese, particularly the Canada Goose, became upland feeders. Some species, such as Brant and Snow, used to feed almost entirely on eel grass, bullrush roots, and sea lettuce. Some 50 years ago, as agriculture expanded, they moved into farming areas for grain.

Goose habitat varies considerably between species. The Nene Goose, which lives only in the mountains of Hawaii, would probably be extinct by now had not Sir Peter Scott obtained a few birds many years ago, and bred them at Slimbridge in England. The experiment was so successful that a regular program of returning birds to the wild has led to a modest recovery. The Blue-winged Goose lives only in the Ethiopian highlands. The Upland Goose lives at high elevations in South America and in the Falkland Islands.

The Canada Goose is certainly the best-known of its family in North America and, perhaps, in the world. Its long black-stocking neck and white chinstrap are familiar to people who might not recognize any other species of goose. In and near cities, these birds have become accustomed to protection. Here they feed and nest in parks, and tolerate the close proximity of people. Geese generally are attracted to urban parks where food is plentiful on the fertilized grassy areas. Indeed, so many have settled in some cities that their droppings foul the lawns. Even in rural areas the Canada Goose now nests close to farms, usually at the edge of ponds and streams, choosing, where possible, firm ground surrounded by water. During the past 30 years or so, the North American population of the Canada Goose has been exploding, both in terms of numbers of birds and of habitat. This has been due, in large part, to thoughtful wildlife management, which includes restoration of wet areas, reduction of bag limits, and the provision of artificial nesting sites in settled areas.

The Canada Goose has developed in the course of its evolution into at least 12 sub-species, ranging in size from the Cackling Goose, which weighs about three pounds, to the Giant Canada Goose which, while averaging 10 to 14 pounds, may sometimes exceed 20 pounds. Geese breeding in the Far North grow progressively smaller. The various sub-species of Canada Goose become darker from east to west.

The Snow Goose comes in two forms: the Greater, which is pure white with black wing tips, and the Lesser, which may be white or blue-grey. These two forms were previously considered to be separate species, but are now recognized as one. The Lesser Snow Goose nests from eastern Siberia, across northern Canada, and migrates through central and western North America. The Greater nests in the extreme northern islands of the Arctic, and migrates through Labrador and the east.

On migration, and in their winter feeding areas, these birds travel and feed in great flocks. One of the most thrilling experiences available to birders is to crouch on the tidal flats on an island in the lower St. Lawrence River when, during their evening flight, thousands of these birds come to land.

With the exception of the Magpie or Pied Goose of Australasia, geese molt their flight feathers after nesting, and cannot fly for about a month. Then they seek open, shallow water for protection and food. The Magpie Goose is unusual in that its long toes are only slightly webbed. It has long, heron-like legs and a long, thin, black neck, rather like a swan's. Its body is black with large, irregular patches of white on the flanks and belly, and it has a yellow face.

The most strongly marked of the geese is the Red-breasted Goose. It ranges across northern Europe, where it nests on the coastal tundra, and wanders in winter as far as Britain, France and Hungary. It is covered with patches of white and red on a black upper body and wings. The most distinctive marking is a large red patch behind the eye, surrounded by a white line. The Emperor Goose of Siberia and Alaska has a lovely ocher-colored head, with a contrasting black throat, pink bill and speckled body.

African Shelduck (*Tadorna cana*)   Living only in South Africa, this
bird has a chestnut-colored body with a white head surmounted by a black
crown. There are, or were, seven species of shelduck, but the Crested
Shelduck of Japan is probably now extinct.

Ruddy Shelduck (*Tadorna ferruginea*)   An attractive chestnut-orange bird, this shelduck ranges from the eastern Mediterranean to eastern Asia. It nests in holes in banks, walls and trees. It is more terrestial than most ducks and can sometimes be found in the arid steppes.

Magellan or Upland Goose (*Chloephaga picta*)   The Magellan Goose lives in the semi-arid plains of the interior of southern Argentina and Chile. In winter it migrates north as far as Buenos Aires. It is also found in the Falkland Islands.

Barnacle Goose (*Branta leucopsis*)   In its breeding areas of the high Arctic of Greenland, Spitzbergen and northern Russia, this goose nests in colonies on rocky ledges and hillsides. In winter it can be seen around the British Isles and the Baltic where it feeds mostly on salt flats.

Brant Goose (*Branta bernicla*)   Like the Canada Goose, the Brant has a black-stocking neck, but its white ring is on the neck below the head. It nests on the arctic coasts of North America, Europe, and Asia, and feeds in salt water farther south in winter.

Cape Barren Goose (*Cereopsis novaehollandiae*)   As the scientific name implies, this goose is native to Australia which was originally known as "New Holland." The handsome blue-gray mantle is dotted with dark spots, and the base of the bill is yellow.

Canada Goose (*Branta canadensis*)   The family of a Canada Goose may consist of up to ten chicks. They may grow at the prodigious rate of almost one pound per week to reach a weight of six or seven pounds in two months.

Right: Canada Goose (*Branta canadensis*)   There are some ten sub-species of the Canada Goose, ranging in size from the three-pound Cackling Goose to the Giant which is known to have reached 24 pounds.

Snow Goose (*Chen caerulescens*)   The Snow Goose winters in the southern
United States and nests in the eastern Arctic. In spring and fall it stops in
the St. Lawrence River east of Quebec City for about a month.

Egyptian Goose (*Alopochen aegyptiaca*)   This relatively small goose is common in ponds and rivers in Africa and Asia Minor. During the rains it extends its range from permanent waters to newly-formed ponds in the plains.

Cape Barren Goose (*Cereopsis novaehollandiae*)   While the Cape Barren Goose
lives in both Australia and New Zealand, it is uncommon in both. This is a
grazing goose, and although a strong swimmer, it seldom enters the water.

Snow Goose (*Chen caerulescens*)   The Snow Goose feeds principally on eel grass, but in winter it may devour grain in cut fields.

White-fronted Goose (*Anser albifrons*)   A circumpolar nester almost
everywhere except in eastern North America, it moves south in winter as
far as Mexico, India, North Africa and Asia. Nesting is often gregarious in
the tundra, deltas and valleys, always close to water.

Greylag Goose (*Anser anser*) There are two forms of the Greylag, the western (found in Britain and western Europe) with an orange bill, and the eastern (found in eastern Europe and Asia) with a pink bill. Some individual birds migrate only locally, while those nesting in Iceland move south.

Magellan or Upland Goose (*Chloephaga picta*) The Magellan Goose may attain a 28-inch wingspan. Its white head and neck, white rump and black barred back are striking.

Emperor Goose (*Philacte canagica*)   The Emperor Goose breeds mostly on the coast of northeastern Siberia and in northwestern Alaska. Some birds straggle south in winter along the coast of western Canada. The pink bill, black throat and white head and neck, set off the strongly-barred body.

Magpie Goose (*Anseranas semipalmata*) The Magpie Goose is unusual in that it does not molt or lose its ability to fly for a period each year. The toes are only partially webbed, the legs very long. It regularly perches in trees. It lives only in Australia and New Guinea.

Orinoco Goose (*Neochen jubata*)   A native of Columbia, Venezuela and the
Guianas, this attractive long-legged goose nests principally on the forested
banks of the Orinoco River and its tributaries.

Pacific White-fronted Goose (*Anser erythropus*)   This is the Asian form of the
White-fronted Goose. It is much browner and somewhat smaller than its
eastern counterpart.

Nene Goose (*Branta sandvicensis*)   This beautiful bird, which nests in the highlands of Hawaii, was close to extinction some 40 years ago. Sir Peter Scott brought a few birds to England where he has built up a breeding flock, returning birds gradually to the wild.

Pink-footed Goose (*Anser brachyrhynchus*)   Their nesting area in Iceland was discovered by Sir Peter Scott. He trekked to the center of the island to band them during the flightless period of the molt. They winter around the British Isles and on the European coasts of the North Sea.

Barnacle Goose (*Branta leucopsis*)   Flocks of Barnacle Geese tend not to
associate with other geese. They can be quarrelsome amongst themselves
and are often noisy. Their call is similar to the yelp of a dog.

Red-breasted Goose (*Bernicla ruficollis*)   This is the most spectacularly marked of all the geese. The heavy body is large in relation to the small head and neck. It is Palearctic and is seen in Asia.

Left: Ross's Goose (*Chen rossii*)   Rather like a diminutive Snow Goose, the Ross's is white with black wingtips (not shown in this photograph). It nests in the low Arctic on the tundra, near fresh-water lakes. It winters principally in central California, and occasionally in Louisiana and Texas.

Snow Goose (*Chen caerulescens*)   The markings of the Snow Goose are shown clearly here: the pure white body, extensive black wingtips and the deep pink on the bill of the male.

White-fronted Goose (*Anser albifrons*)   On its circumpolar breeding grounds the White-fronted Goose often nests in loose colonies. The four to six eggs are laid in a down-filled nest on the ground. The female incubates while the male stands guard during the four weeks that they take to hatch.

Shelduck (*Tadorna tadorna*) From a distance the Shelduck appears to be black-and-white, despite the strong coloring that can be seen at close quarters. It is widespread on the coasts of Britain, Europe, North Africa and Asia. It often nests in rabbit warrens and bushes near the shores.

Snow Goose (*Chen caerulescens*)   The Snow Goose comes in two phases, blue and white. Western birds are mixed blue and white, while the eastern birds are white only. This appears to be a first-year bird in the blue phase. As they age the bill turns pink.

Swan Goose (*Anser cygnoides*)   The breeding range of the Swan Goose is central Siberia, east to the Kamchatka and Commander islands, and south into Mongolia. It is almost always seen close to water, whether in mountain rivers or on the sea.

Magellan or Upland Goose (*Chloephaga picta*) On pages 40 and 51 there are pictures of the Magellan Goose which show a distinct break between the white head and black neck and breast. The birds seen here are not in breeding plumage and vary considerably.

DUCKS

Australian Wood Duck (*Chenonetta jubata*)   In Australia this bird is also known as the Maned Goose because of its long neck and legs. The brown head and strong markings of the male on the right contrast with the more sober female.

There are about 127 species of ducks in the world. They appear almost everywhere, with the exception of Antarctica, the Sahara, central Greenland and central Australia. Some, like the Wood Duck, the Harlequin and the Baikal Teal are brilliantly colored, while others, including the Black Duck of North America and the Grey Teal of Australasia, are mottled and rather drab. In weight, they range from the tiny teal at well under a pound, to the Common Eider at over five pounds. The wings are short and pointed, with the high ratio of weight-to-wing area making it necessary for them to pump their wings continuously and fast to remain airborne. Even at a considerable distance, it is possible to tell a duck from a goose in flight, but it requires considerable experience to tell one duck from another.

Ornithologists divide families of birds (in this case the Anatidae, being all the swans, geese and ducks) into sub-families and the sub-families into tribes, of which there are 11. These 11 tribes are further subdivided into 43 *genera*. Some of these *genera* have only one or two members, while others have many. The dabbling ducks, for instance, are of the genus Anas, of which there are 46 species. (Dabbling ducks are those that up-end and feed with only their heads and necks below the surface of the water). Examples of dabbling duck are the Mallard, Pintail, teal and wigeon. The diving ducks, or those that take their food while swimming under the surface, mostly in fresh water, are called Aythyini, and include the North American Canvasback and pochards or scaup. There are, in addition, some 20 species of sea ducks, or Mergini, which feed mostly in the oceans. They include the mergansers, eiders, and scoters. Next there are eight species of stifftail, Oxyurini, including the Black-headed Duck of South America, the Ruddy Duck of North America, and the Blue-billed Duck of Australia. Other tribes of duck are the Freckled Duck (one species), steamer ducks (three species), and perching ducks (13 species). The various species of each *genus* will have more characteristics in common than those at the base of the family tree.

Ducks generally have shorter necks than geese or swans. They molt, usually twice each year, lose their ability to fly while molting, have webbed feet, and in most cases have wide, flat bills. Most are more mobile on the water than on land. Within the range of these generalizations, the habits and appearance of the species differ widely. The most fundamental difference in habit is the method of feeding. One group takes all or most of its food while swimming under water, and the other group feeds either on land, or by up-ending and feeding just below the surface of the water.

Among the first group we find the sea ducks and bay ducks such as the eiders, Harlequin, Oldsquaw, scoter, Bufflehead, merganser, scaup, pochard and steamer ducks. In the more land-oriented group, are the whistling ducks, and dabblers. There is a further tendency for those ducks that feed under water to take a higher ratio of animal matter in the form of molluscs, crustacea and fish, than of vegetable matter. On the other hand, many adult dabblers are almost entirely vegetarian, although the young feed on insects when they are growing.

Diving ducks are divided into three tribes, and further subdivided into 12 *genera* worldwide. They have evolved with special skills for diving and remaining submerged for fairly long periods. The legs are set near the rear of the body, which facilitates swimming under the surface. A few species, including mergansers, also use their wings to swim. On land they are clumsy, at best able to shuffle along, often pushing themselves on their breasts. As a consequence, most diving and bay ducks nest as close as possible to water, although some, such as Common Mergansers, Hooded Mergansers and Goldeneyes, nest in cavities in trees many feet above the ground. When the young of cavity-nesting ducks hatch, they scramble in turn to the entrance, and tumble to the ground. The female then leads them to water. The young develop quickly, but still require nearly two months before they are capable of flying.

Diving ducks are well adapted to their environment. The location of the legs and webbed feet, near the rear of the body, give them strong propulsion under the surface; their lungs and metabolism are such that they can remain submerged for several minutes. The sea ducks, in particular, can reach their prey below the surface. Most, including the scaup, scoters and eiders have wide, flat bills.

The mergansers, however, have sharp, pointed bills. The sides of the bills are strongly serrated, enabling them to hold struggling fish. They are carnivorous, feeding mostly on fish, but also on eels, frogs and insects. Mergansers are unpopular on fishing rivers and lakes, although sometimes without cause. If coarse fish and game fish are both present, mergansers will concentrate on the more sluggish fish that compete for food with game fish. If only game fish are present, as is often the case in Atlantic salmon rivers, mergansers may do considerable damage to the stock of young.

Dabbling ducks, and other species that feed in shallow water and on land, are considerably more agile out of the water. They are capable of diving, but do so only when alarmed or when escaping from danger. For example, Bald Eagles and Peregrine Falcons often harass ducks, forcing them to dive time after time until they are exhausted, and can be picked up on the surface.

It is the dabbling ducks that take the greatest pressure from shooting, for their flesh is more palatable than others. Ducks that feed largely on fish and other animal matter tend to have a strong flavor.

The Mallard is probably the most abundant and widespread of the Anas group, for it lives from the Arctic areas of Europe, Asia and North America, to the sub-tropics. It is also the most heavily shot. It has been calculated that about 70 percent of young Mallards in North America die in their first year, about half from shooting, and half from other causes. When one considers that less than half of the nesting pairs are successful in producing young, one might wonder how the species can survive, but it does. Continued survival of all duck species relies on their capacity to lay large numbers of eggs (average 9 or 10 for most species) and their usual habit of nesting a second time if the first nest fails. Habitat loss in settled areas through drainage and drought is a more compelling pressure than shooting, although, as already mentioned, this situation has stabilized to some extent during the past quarter century.

In North America, governments, and private agencies like Ducks Unlimited, have done much to bring back marginal agricultural land into wetland. Significant areas have been set aside and protected, water has been impounded and controlled, and suitable plants introduced.

The vast majority of ducks, particularly those in the Northern Hemisphere, migrate. In areas like Australia and Africa, where there are seasonal periods of drought, ducks may only move far enough to find water. In a country such as New Zealand, where water is relatively plentiful, migration is quite limited. In the Northern Hemisphere, it would appear that the strongest urge to travel the huge distances to the Arctic and back comes from a little-understood need for light, as well as suitable food.

Most species of waterfowl breeding in the Northern Hemisphere nest in a wide band, from the high Arctic, to southern North America and Europe. It is not known why some Mallards in North America, for example, choose the northern limits of Alaska, and others choose Texas. It is known, however, that this bird with a North American breeding population fluctuating between 6 million and more than 13 million, centers its breeding activity in the Canadian prairies. The Oldsquaw, a long-tailed diving duck, nests only in the Arctic.

Most ducks travel principally over land and can, if they choose, rest and feed along the way. Some travel great distances over water. Losses from choosing this route are probably high. Some Blue-winged Teal, for instance, fly from the northern United States to South America — some 2,500 miles. One immature Blue-winged Teal is recorded as having flown 3,800 miles from the Athabasca Delta in Manitoba, Canada, to Venezuela, in one month.

The average speed at which a duck flies on migration is about 50 miles per hour. This suggests that some non-stop flights over water would take from 40 to 50 hours. Pintails, Lesser Scaup and wigeon bred in Alaska turn up in the Hawaiian islands. Most ducks and geese travel on migration at heights of 1,000 to 3,000 feet, although many go much higher. Sea ducks, such as eiders and scoters, travel much lower, often only a few feet above the water.

Sea ducks are generally chunky birds with thick, impervious down. On the ocean, one can often see them raising themselves in the water and flapping their wings. These birds may spend the whole winter at sea coming to land only to nest. They are killed for food only by native people in the Far North. Their flesh is somewhat unpalatable. Olds-quaws, which are handsome black-and-white sea ducks, winter in both fresh and salt water in Europe, North America and around Japan.

The stifftails are small duck, with short, fanned tails of stiff feathers. They are reddish-colored and have blue bills. They take all their food, primarily vegetable with some animal matter, while swimming along the bottom and sifting it in their bills. In North and South America, this tribe is represented by the Ruddy Duck and the Masked Duck, and in Australia by the Blue-billed Duck.

Among the ducks, the drake remains with the hen only during the egg-laying period, often deserting before the clutch is complete. Thus, the hen must incubate and care for the young alone — the drake having moved off with other males in preparation for the molt. During the molt, the male loses his nuptial plumage, and soon cannot be readily distinguished from the hen. Molting ducks are flightless for a period, usually about 30 days.

The courtship behavior of ducks is not as elaborate, in most cases, as among grebes, but males are assiduous in keeping other males away from their mates. Males do display, however, with movements and posturing that best show their iridescent speculum on the wing. This is particularly true of the dabbling ducks.

White-cheeked or Bahama Pintail (*Anas bahamensis*)   Although this bird
appears to be quite pale, most birds of this species are mottled brown above
and below, while only the cheeks and neck are white. It nests from the
Bahamas south through the West Indies and is widespread in South
America to Chile.

Common Eider (*Somateria mollissima*) The Eider chicks seen here are in a nest of down pulled from the breast of the mother. The collectors of down on the cliffs in Scandinavia now take only part of the nest lining and, as a consequence, do not interfere unduly with the eggs or young.

Left: Black-bellied Whistling Duck (*Dendrocygna autumnalis*)   Formerly known as "Tree ducks," members of this tribe are now called "Whistling ducks." The Black-bellied Whistling Duck perches readily in trees and ranges from Texas to Argentina.

Gadwall (*Anas strepera*)   The Gadwall is widely distributed in North America, Europe and Asia, but is not common. It does not venture into the Arctic, preferring mid-latitude nesting sites. Despite its rather drab appearance here, it is a finely marked, elegant bird, with a white patch on the wing.

Barrow's Goldeneye (*Bucephala islandica*)   Breeding in Iceland, Greenland, Labrador, and in the western part of North America from Alaska to California, this duck does not wander far from its nesting area in winter. It nests in a hollow tree or in cavities in stream banks or, sometimes, under the overhang of boulders.

Right: American Black Duck (*Anas Rubipes*)   A large, dark duck, common in eastern Canada and the United States, the American Black Duck breeds from northern Labrador south to Virginia and Ohio. Seen here in molt, this bird will be unable to fly for about a month. It grows new flight feathers for its autumn migration to southern Canada and the United States.

Blue Duck (*Hymenoliamus malacorhynchos*)   New Zealand was once connected to Australia as part of a huge continent, and many bird and insect species are common to both countries. This little duck, however, occurs only in New Zealand.

Bufflehead (*Bucephala albeola*)   The male Bufflehead shown here is in spring plumage. The female is more subdued and has a white patch behind the eye. It nests in holes in trees from Quebec to Alaska and south to northern California.

Common Eider (*Somateria mollissima*) One of the largest of all ducks, the Common Eider can withstand storms and bitterly cold weather with ease. It nests from northern Russia to Ireland and Maine, and winters in the Atlantic and northern Pacific.

American Black Duck (*Anas rubipes*) This is a large duck of the ponds and marshes of eastern North America. It is a dabbler that up-ends while feeding on grasses and other plants below the surface.

Common Goldeneye (*Bucephala clangula*)   The Common Goldeneye breeds in northern forests around the world, building its nest in hollow trees. It is also known as a "whistler" because of the loud whistle made by the wings as it flies.

Harlequin Duck (*Histrionicus histrionicus*)   A beautiful, intricately marked
and colorful duck, the Harlequin nests from eastern Siberia to both coastal
areas of North America. It nests near swift rivers and winters in the ocean,
usually feeding in turbulent water near rocks.

Fulvous Whistling Duck (*Dendrocygna bicolor*)   There are several disjunctive regions where this bird lives: in India and Burma; in the Arabian peninsula; in eastern Africa; in parts of South America, the southern United States, and in Mexico. From these nesting areas it wanders, usually singly, as far north as southern Canada.

Canvasback (*Aythya valisineria*)   Named for its whitish back, the Canvasback nests in prairie potholes of western North America, although it may be seen on migration in the east. It dives for its food, usually in shallow water.

Right: King Eider (*Somateria spectabilis*)   At sea, where it winters as far north as it can find open water, the King Eider is one of the deepest-diving of all ducks. Dives of 180 feet are not uncommon. It feeds almost entirely on animal matter, but females and young eat some buds and leaves when the young are growing.

Left: Canvasback (*Aythya valisineria*)   In dry years the Canvasback, which needs more water than most prairie nesting species in North America, is hard hit. During the dry 1930s the North American population declined dramatically and took many years to recover.

Fulvous Whistling Duck (*Dendrocygna bicolor*)   The relatively small population of this duck in the United States nests, for the most part, on the levees of rice fields in Texas and Louisiana. Unlike most ducks, both parents assist in raising the young. They are nocturnal feeders.

Mallard (*Anas platyrhynchos*) Here we see the rather drab hen with young.
It is usual for 10 or more eggs to be laid, of which some do not hatch, and
more are lost before the young birds reach the flying stage. Only the large
clutches allow the species to survive.

Ring-necked Duck (*Aythya collaris*)   The female seen here is very similar to the male during the mid-stage of the prenuptial molt. It is also quite similar to the scaups, although slightly smaller, and with a rounder head. On the wing it darts about, rather like a teal.

Mallard (*Anas platyrhynchos*) The bird in the left foreground has its wings set in the downward curve for landing. On taking off from the water Mallards leap straight into the air and are flying immediately.

Comb Duck (*Sarkidiornis melanotos*) A native of northern South America, Africa and Asia, the Comb Duck resembles the Muscovy Duck which, however, has a black head. This bird up-ends, dives and grazes for its food, mostly grain and shoots, but sometimes frogs and insects.

Right: Mandarin Duck (*Aix gelericulata*) This gorgeous bird is a native of the Far East, China, Manchuria, Taiwan and Japan. It is a favorite in zoos all over the world because of its spectacular markings and color.

Preceding pages: Oldsquaw (*Clangula hyemalis*)   A resident of both hemispheres, the Oldsquaw winters in open water, both fresh and salt. It is a diver, feeding on small fish and crustacea. In the spring it migrates northward, nesting as far north as the land goes.

Wood Duck (*Aix sponsa*)   Considered by many the most beautiful of all ducks, the Wood Duck nests in holes in trees, and in nesting boxes if they are available. It may often be seen perched high in trees.

Musk Duck (*Biziura lobata*)   On a pond in Australia or Tasmania, its home, the Musk Duck is often hard to recognize as a bird. It flaps about, looking more like an active turtle. It is fairly common in swamps, lakes and rivers.

New Zealand Shelduck (*Tadorna variegata*)   Widely distributed on both islands of New Zealand, the New Zealand Shelduck nests near ponds, either on the ground or in hollow trees.

Black-bellied Whistling Duck (*Dendrocygna autumnalis*)   In flight whistling ducks flap their wings relatively slowly looking more like geese than ducks, the legs trailing behind the tail. They then whistle frequently. Some whistling ducks congregate in large flocks, though the Black-bellied is seldom seen in groups of more than a few birds.

Northern Shoveler (*Anas clypeata*)   The markings on this North American duck are similar to those of the Mallard. The Shoveler is named for its flat, over-sized bill. It is a dabbling duck.

Left: Northern Pintail (*Anas acuta*)   The Northern Pintail is probably the second most abundant duck in North America, after the Mallard, and has the widest distribution worldwide of any of the waterfowl. The photograph does not show the long pointed tail, nor the elegant pointed stripe running down the back of the neck.

Torrent Duck (*Merganetta armata*)   The Torrent Duck shown here is in a typical setting — a racing river where it can maintain position in a roaring current. It seldom flies. It occurs from Columbia to Terra del Fuego only at elevations above 6,000 feet.

Water Whistling Duck (*Dendrocygna arcuata*)   The Water Whistling Duck is
widely distributed throughout the southwest Pacific as far as Australia. This
bird was photographed at Cairns in the northeast corner of Australia. It
prefers lakes and lagoons where it dives for its food, usually to about 10 feet.
It also dabbles, taking water lily seed and buds.

Ring-necked Duck (*Aythya collaris*) The male Ring-necked Duck shown here is in full nuptial plumage. The name is inappropriate, for the brown ring on the neck is scarcely discernable, even at close range. This species nests to about 60 degrees north latitude in North America, and winters around the Caribbean.

Northern Pintail (*Anas acuta*)   In North America vast numbers of Pintails nest on the prairies, and the range extends north to the Arctic Ocean. Most North American birds winter in the western Caribbean.

Ruddy Duck (*Oxyura jamaicensis*)   The Ruddy Duck is a North American member of the Stifftail group, so known because of its fanned spiky tail feathers. It dives to the bottom and feeds by sifting animal and vegetable matter through its wide bill.

Left: Tufted Duck (*Aythya fuligula*)   Similar in appearance to the scaups, the Tufted Duck nests throughout Europe, including Iceland, close to lakes and ponds. This is a sociable bird, often joining domestic flocks in parks. Partially migratory, some individuals move south to Africa and Asia.

Smew (*Mergus albellus*)   A mostly-white duck of the "sawbill" group, the Smew nests in the extreme north of Europe and Russia. It migrates to most of central Europe where it winters in rivers and lakes and along the coasts. It nests in hollow trees.

Redhead (*Aythya americana*)   This picture shows the contrast between the strongly-marked male Redhead in nuptial plumage and the rather subdued female. Most Redheads pair in the autumn, remain together during the winter and until the nest is full. The male then departs. This is a North American bird nesting almost entirely in the central plains.

Right: Redhead (*Aythya americana*)   The young of Redheads suffer severe mortality, usually about 80 percent, due to predation and hunting. The population ranges between 600,000 and 900,000 birds depending on breeding conditions in the prairies.

American Wigeon (*Anas americana*)   The principal nesting area of the
American Wigeon is in the pothole country of Saskatchewan and Alberta,
although some birds go as far north as the Arctic Ocean. They migrate
outward and south to the western United States, the Atlantic seaboard, and
the Caribbean.

White-faced Whistling Duck (*Dendrocygna viduata*) The White-faced
Whistling duck is now reported to be very rare in Costa Rica and Panama,
and is more common in the tropical parts of South America. It also occurs in
Madagascar and some parts of Africa. It is often seen with groups of Black-
bellied Whistling Ducks.

Left: Common Merganser (*Mergus merganser*)   A bird with Holarctic distribution in fairly temperate latitudes north of the equator, the Common Merganser, or Sawbill, is a diver, living entirely on small fish and other animal matter. Those shown here are juveniles which have the same markings as the adult females.

Hooded Merganser (*Mergus cucullatus*)   The Hooded Merganser is the only merganser indigenous to North America. The whole population does not exceed 100,000 birds. They nest in tree cavities where hatchlings remain for about a day before heading for the water.

Red-breasted Merganser (*Mergus serrator*)   All mergansers have the ability to float low in the water like the male Red-breasted Merganser shown here. A bird of the Northern Hemisphere around the world, it nests in northern forests and tundra, and winters mostly in salt water.

American Wigeon (*Anas americana*)   The two male American Wigeons shown here are in full spring plumage. One appears to be driving the other off, perhaps to keep it away from its mate. Territorial protection is strong in nesting ducks.

Yellow-billed Duck (*Anas undulata*)   Quite a large duck, resident only in Africa from Angola to Ethiopia and south to South Africa, the Yellow-billed Duck is uncommon and local. It is decreasing in numbers throughout its range where it lives in fresh water lakes, marshes and pools. It is a dabbler, up-ending for its food, which consists mostly of seeds and shoots.

Red-crested Pochard (*Netta rufina*)   The Red-crested Pochard breeds intermittently in Europe and central Asia on reedy fresh-water lakes and lagoons. It is seldom seen on salt water. After nesting the male loses his handsome appearance and resembles the rather drab female.

Left: European Wigeon (*Anas penelope*)   The European Wigeon is not unlike the American Wigeon, but has a yellow forehead — the American's is white. It nests from Iceland, Scotland and northern Europe to Asia. It winters mostly in salt water and feeds in shallows and mud flats. Occasional birds stray to North America.

European Wigeon (*Anas penelope*)   The European Wigeon shown here is a female. It resembles the male, but is smaller, has a more rounded head, and a rosier coloring.

Rosy-billed Pochard (*Netta peposaca*)   A South American species, the Rosy-
billed Pochard lives from southern Brazil through Uruguay, Paraguay,
Argentina to Chile. Note the pronounced nob at the base of the bill and the
fiery red eye.

Auckland Island Teal (*Anas aucklandica*)   The Auckland Island Teal is also known as the Auckland Island Flightless Duck. This drab brown bird is a native of New Zealand and occurs nowhere else.

Lesser Scaup (*Aythya affinis*)   A North American species, the Lesser Scaup population varies between five and 10 million birds. It nests from the central plains and California north to the Bering Sea, with the greatest concentration in the Northwest Territories.

Green-winged Teal (*Anas crecca carolinensis*)   The average weight of the Green-winged Teal is about 12 ounces. It nests from the Aleutian Islands, the tundra, the prairies to Quebec and, rarely, the northwestern United States. The male seen here is in breeding plumage.

Ringed Teal (*Anas leucorphrys*)   The Ringed Teal lives from the Matto Grosso in Brazil, south through Uruguay, Paraguay, Bolivia and Argentina. The back of the female is similar to that of the male seen here, but the top of the head is brown and there is a line below the eye on the pale cheeks.

Cape Wigeon (*Anas capensis*)   Generally pale in appearance, the Cape
Wigeon lives in Africa, with the greatest concentration in the soda and
brackish lakes of the Rift Valley. Its principal distinguishing feature is the
bright pink bill.

Chestnut Teal (*Anas castanea*)   The Chestnut Teal lives only in Tasmania and Australia where it frequents both fresh and brackish marshes and ponds. It is a cavity-nesting bird that will use nesting boxes readily.

Cinnamon Teal (*Anas cyanoptera*)   There are five races of Cinnamon Teal of which four live in South America as far south as Argentina, and the other nests in the western United States and southern British Columbia. The male, seen here, is vividly colored.

Garganey Teal (*Anas querquedula*)   The Garganey Teal has a wide distribution from southeast England, across central Europe, Africa, Asia and Indonesia. It is a migrant in the southern part of this range. The female does not have the blue side patch of the male, seen here, and its eye stripe is not as pronounced.

Left: Chestnut Teal (*Anas castanea*)   A pair of Chestnut Teal may have two or even three clutches, each consisting of about nine or 10 eggs, in the course of their long breeding season.

Baikal Teal (*Anas formosa*)   The Baikal Teal is native to the taiga of northern
and northeastern Siberia. It has been seen occasionally in Britain and
western Europe, but normally migrates south through Manchuria and Korea
to Japan and southeastern China, sometimes reaching northern India and
Siam.

Blue-winged Teal (*Anas discors*)   The Blue-winged Teal breeds mainly in the pothole country of the North American prairies. Nests are made in long grass as much as a mile from water. The five million or so teal of this species migrate to the southern United States, the Caribbean, and South America.

Lesser Scaup (*Aythya affinis*) Breeding only in North America, from Alaska
to northern Ontario and south to the central prairies, the Lesser Scaup is
the most numerous North American diving duck with a population that
ranges between five and nine million. It prefers to nest near potholes and
lakes at least 10 feet deep.

Surf Scoter (*Melanitta perspicillata*)   A North American species that nests in the northern forested country from Alaska to Quebec. It winters on both oceans as far south as Baja California in the west and Florida in the east. Migration is mainly by sea, although some birds are seen on the Great Lakes in winter.

Greater Scaup (*Aythya marila*)   Compare the white body feathers of this bird with the rather darker Lesser Scaup shown on page 128. The Greater Scaup nests in tundra and boreal forests around the northern edges of the Northern Hemisphere. In North America it breeds only in western Alaska and near the mouth of the Mackenzie River.

GREBES AND CORMORANTS

Double-crested Cormorant (*Phalacrocorax auritus*) There are 20 species of cormorant living in all parts of the temperate and tropical world where there are fish to eat. The Double-crested is common in North America from Alaska south in summer; it winters in Honduras.

Strictly speaking, grebes and cormorants do not fall into the family of waterfowl, but they share the same habitat and are often seen together in both fresh and salt water. It is for this reason, and for purposes of comparison, that we include a description of them here.

The grebes are a family of 20 species of waterbirds divided into six *genera*. They occur on all continents, except Antarctica, as far north as the Arctic Ocean, and as far south as the tips of the southern continents. All species nest on fresh water, on lakes, ponds, slow-flowing rivers and marshes. Outside of the nesting season, some long-necked and elegant Western Grebes of the Pacific coast of North America, for example, feed in salt water.

Many people, who have never noticed a grebe in the wild have seen them on film, for their elaborate courtship display is a favorite subject of nature programs. There one sees the grebe raise itself, leaving only the stern in the water, and paddle furiously along in an upright position. With the exception of the Pied-billed, grebes have sharp, longish bills, and relatively long necks. Grebes' toes are not webbed, but have flexible lobes which add propulsion and direction while swimming. The ankles and toes are so jointed that they can turn in any direction. All grebes are almost entirely carnivorous: they feed on insects, crustacea and some molluscs which they take, for the most part, under water. Grebes are superbly adapted to life in the water. They are buoyant, but have the capacity to expel the air from their feathers, by compacting them and emptying their air sacs. This allows them to float low in the water, when they choose, or to sink below the surface. Their 20,000 or so feathers are impervious to water.

The legs of grebes are located so far back on the body that they are virtually incapable of walking, or even of standing upright. As a consequence, they nest in soggy masses of floating vegetation, usually concealed by rushes or grass, and anchored to them. The female lays from two to six eggs, which she incubates from three weeks to a month. When hatched, the chicks ride about clinging to the back of the parent, and remain there when the parent dives.

Several species, including the Slavonian or Horned and Black-necked or Eared Grebes, have elaborate crests which may extend under the chin. These are raised during courtship with headshaking and the presentation of a bundle of weeds.

The northern nesting species, including the Horned and Red-necked, undertake long flights on migration. Since the tail is no more than a tuft of small feathers, grebes do not maneuver well. During the nesting season, they seldom take to the air. When they do, they require a long, paddling run for take-off. A few South American species have lost the ability to fly and are, as a consequence, limited to the areas in which they live. Should their habitat change, either through natural or imposed conditions, they are threatened. One, the Colombian Grebe, is probably now extinct and another, the Atitlan, which breeds only on the lake of that name in Guatemala, is threatened by the possible development of a hydroelectric site. When in danger, grebes do not fly, but either dive or sink, and then swim to the protection of the reeds.

Three species, the Horned or Slavonian, the Eared or Black-necked, and the Red-necked, are widely distributed on both sides of the Atlantic. The Least lives from the southern reaches of Texas and Mexico to Argentina, and is common throughout the West Indies. The Great Crested and Little Grebe range from Europe and Africa to Australasia. The grebe most commonly seen in the ponds and marshes of the North American prairies is the Pied-billed, a small stubby-billed bird, known for its slurred whistling notes. The range of brays, chatterings, squeals, grunts and croaks produced by grebes is astonishing, especially in the pre-dawn, when the marsh might otherwise be quite quiet. In the north, Horned or Red-necked grebes are most common.

The 29 species of cormorants are closely related to the pelicans, gannets, tropicbirds, frigatebirds and darters. All have mostly drab black or brown feathers, but some have white on their underparts, and some color on facial patches. The Romans named them *corvus marinus* or, in English "sea raven." This passed through the French as *cor marin*, hence in English to "cormorant."

Cormorants dive for their food from the surface. They push themselves upward with their feet and arch gracefully into the water where they chase their prey. They are wonderfully agile under water: they use their powerful legs for propulsion, while their wings remain tightly by their sides. They feed on small fish at various depths, but it is likely that bottom-feeding fish make up the bulk of the diet for most cormorant species. Cormorants are capable of remaining submerged for a matter of minutes, and of reaching depths of about 200 feet. Most, however, feed in relatively shallow water, fairly close to shore.

These birds have huge appetites. In feeding, they convert protein into nitrates and phosphates in prodigious quantities, enriching the quality of their feeding grounds. Most species have a beneficial effect in that they feed on small fish of no commercial value. Off the coasts of Peru and Chile, however, millions of Guanay Cormorants compete with fishermen for the anchovy catch. It is the Guanays that are most responsible for the flourishing industry which converts the huge quantities of dried guano collected from the islands into fertilizer.

Cormorants, or Shags as some species are called, nest in colonies, sometimes consisting of only a few pairs, but more often numbering in the hundreds. They seek areas, often islands, that afford protection from predators. Some colonies are shared with other seabirds; in Australia and New Zealand several species of cormorant often nest together. Nests must be in a windy place or at the edge of a cliff, for these birds are incapable of walking without tripping, let alone running for take-off. At a crowded site, these birds are unstable, both on landing, and when they are at the nest. Each species has developed signals to indicate its intentions to other nesters. When a bird is about to leave the nest, it opens its mouth to show that its plans are not aggressive. Olivaceous and Double-crested cormorants, which sometimes nest in trees, have great problems landing safely.

When the young of cormorants hatch they are, unlike those of waterfowl, blind and naked. In about two weeks, they are covered with thick down, and in a further five or six weeks, they can fly. During this period, each parent makes many trips to the nest with food.

The feathers of cormorants are permeable, so the skin becomes wet when they dive. Consequently, the birds have to dry their wings after a number of dives. Cormorants can often be seen with wings outstretched in the sun. Even the Galapagos Cormorant, which long ago lost the power to fly, stretches its rudimentary wings. This habit may also have a temperature-control function. Their dark feathers absorb heat from the sun which must, on occasion, be dispelled by panting. The air passes through the throat pouch, which is rich in blood vessels, and cools the bird.

Cormorants are like pelicans in that all four toes are connected by a web. With ducks and geese, only three toes are connected. Again, unlike waterfowl that have the capacity to store fat in their bodies as insulation and energy for long journeys, cormorants are lean. This limits their range to water that is reasonably temperate.

Several species, including the Olivaceous and Double-crested cormorants, nest both on fresh and salt water but some, including the White-necked Cormorant of Africa, appear to live entirely on fresh water. New colonies appear and others are deserted, particularly on island lakes. One colony of Double-crested Cormorants at Lake of the Woods in western Ontario, is more than one thousand miles from salt water and has been colonized during the past few years where there was none before.

In flight, cormorants can be distinguished from ducks by a slower lumbering wingbeat, and by the hump-backed appearance caused by carrying the long neck slightly lower than the line of the back.

Left: Pied Cormorant (*Phalacrocorax varius*)   Known in Australia and New Zealand, where it lives, as the Yellow-faced Cormorant, the Pied Cormorant has a white throat, chest and belly. It nests in colonies in flooded areas, preferring to locate directly over the water.

Eared Grebe (*Podiceps nigricollis*)   The Eared Grebe, known in Europe as the Black-necked, is the smallest of the 20 grebe species. Note the chick peeping out from the back. Although the young can swim, they often ride and dive clinging to the mother's back.

Pied-billed Grebe (*Podilymbus podiceps*)   Restricted to the Western
Hemisphere, the Pied-billed Grebe lives from the prairie provinces of
Canada, south to southern Argentina. It nests in pairs, building a floating
nest of rank vegetation. The young leave the nest within hours of hatching.
Note the stout short bill.

Right: Horned Grebe (*Podiceps auritus*)   The Horned, or Slavonian Grebe, as it
is known in Europe, is Holarctic. It breeds in northern Europe and Iceland
and in North America from southern Alaska, south to the central prairies of
the United States. It is not a colonial nester and one usually finds only one
pair on each pond.

Galapagos Cormorant (*Nannopterum harrisi*)   Also known as the Flightless
Cormorant, it lives only in the Galapagos where, after thousands of years of
freedom from predators, it lost the need to fly. Its wings are vestigial, ragged
things. With the introduction of rats and dogs, this cormorant is now in
danger of extinction.

Eared Grebe (*Podiceps nigricollis*)   The sharp bill of the Eared Grebe appears to be tilted upward because of the slope of the lower mandible. In full breeding plumage the throat is black and the fan of feathers behind the eye is golden.

Following page: Red-necked Grebe (*Podiceps griseigena*)   Holarctic, the Red-necked Grebe nests north of the Great Lakes, across western Canada and Alaska, northern Asia and eastern Europe. The male bird is shown here incubating. The Eared Grebe nests on fresh water but winters close to shore, mostly in salt water.

PHOTOGRAPH CREDITS

INDEX TO PHOTOGRAPHS